I0837431

Introduction

I'm very happy and excited to dedicate this book, to all those seeking to create loving, fulfilling and enduring relationships! Every page of this book offers 'powerful' and 'profound' relationship secrets and ideas, you can use, to create truly joyful and fulfilling relationships. There are 261 unique ideas presented in this book. Each idea has the unique potential to transform your thinking and alter the very way, you view and approach relationships! The ideas presented are truly universal and can be applied to any relationship you wish to improve and enhance - whether it's your relationship with your- wife, husband, boyfriend, girlfriend, son, daughter, father, mother, brother, sister, friend, uncle, aunt, boss, co-worker or whoever!

As you go through the pages of this book, please allow time for the true meaning and profoundness of each idea, to sink into your consciousness. Soaking yourself in the depth and essence of the ideas presented, will not only help you embody their essence but will also help you express them in your relationships every day, with power, conviction and emotion!   I recommend you read one 'Power' thought' each day in the morning, when you wake up or in the night, before you go to bed.

Spend five or ten minutes to contemplate the essence of each 'Power Thought' and visualize the results you desire to see in your relationship. See in your mind what you want and feel as though, what you want in your relationship has already become a reality! You can do this as many times as you want in a day and even write down the desired results you wish to see in your relationship!

It's my earnest desire that, you understand and imbibe the true essence of each idea presented in this book and take positive action to make the ideas a 'reality'!

I have no doubt; the ideas will create a transformational shift in your thinking and I'm confident you'll combine the shift in thinking with positive action and emotion to manifest the desired outcomes you wish to see in your relationships!

Wishing you the very best of life, filled with the most loving, joyful, fulfilling and enduring relationships!

With Love,

Roy John

1

There is no life without Relationships. Your relationship with yourself, people and everything around you determines the quality of your life!

<u>2</u>

The more you enjoy your relationships, the more you'll enjoy life. Go the fullest depth possible in your relationships to enjoy life to the fullest!

Ultimate Secrets To Great Relationships

By

ROY JOHN

<u>3</u>

People and things around you, provide an opportunity for the 'true' nature of your soul to flower and blossom!

<u>4</u>

When you enjoy giving without conditions, you enjoy the purest form of love in a relationship!

5

Don't look for 'Love' in a relationship. Be the 'Love' you are looking for and you'll be lovable and loved!

<u>6</u>

Whether you live in a 'loving' or 'unloving' world has nothing to do with the world. It entirely depends on your relationship with it!

7

You cannot be a true 'Friend' in a relationship if you always listen with your 'head' and never with your 'heart'!

<u>8</u>

We often hurt those who love us and go out of our way to please and praise those we hardly know. Remember, people who love us deserve more of our 'love' and 'thoughtfulness'!

9

Stop expecting the person in your relationship to be 100% perfect and start accepting them for who they are. No one is 100% perfect (including yourself)!

10

Your joy in a relationship depends on how much you 'give'. Look for more ways to 'give'!

11

The best way to deepen your relationship with someone is to deepen your understanding of the person. The best way to understand a person is by listening and careful observation!

<u>12</u>

Every person on this planet has a strong and unquestionable need to belong. A 'loving' and 'inclusive' relationship is the only way you can fulfill this need!

13

In a true relationship you don't try to walk 'ahead' or 'behind' someone. You walk 'with' the person like a true friend!

<u>14</u>

When you focus on what you are 'getting', you suck the juice out of your relationship. When you focus on what you are 'giving', you keep your relationship 'juicy'!

15

Relationship is like a Bank. The more deposits you make into it, the more you can withdraw in times of need!

16

Keep this fundamental relationship rule etched in your heart: Never 'say' or 'do' anything in a relationship you'll never 'say' or 'do' to yourself!

17

There is no 'right' or 'wrong' in a relationship. Your ability to see the other viewpoint, adds more depth and meaning to your relationship!

<u>18</u>

Relationships thrive

where there is flow of 'positive' energy. 'Acceptance' and 'Forgiveness' keeps positive energy flowing in your relationship!

19

It's not about being 'right'. It's about being 'kind. When faced with a choice, always choose to be 'kind' in your relationship!

<u>20</u>

Relationships are made of 'emotional' bonds not 'logical' bonds. Build strong emotional bonds to build strong relationships!

<u>21</u>

Pay attention to things that bother you in a relationship. They'll often lead you to things 'within' yourself that need healing!

<u>22</u>

Friends and Relationships greatly influence the quality of your life. Choose them wisely!

<u>23</u>

The greatest gift you can bring into a relationship is your willingness to focus on 'agreements' instead of 'disagreements'!

24

You are 100% responsible for the 'health' of your relationship. Love is the nutrient that keeps it healthy!

25

Give your best love today. There is no guarantee you'll get a chance to give your best love tomorrow!

<u>26</u>

The Love you 'withhold' is lost forever. The Love you 'give' is forever gained!

27

The most important relationship in the world is your relationship with yourself. All other relationships are just an extension of this relationship!

28

The best way into a person's heart is through things they love and admire. Talking and doing things they love and admire, is a sure-fire way into their heart!

<u>29</u>

Be an 'Encourager' and not a 'Critic' in your relationship. Encouragement strengthens your relationship, while Criticism weakens it!

30

The true measure of your love in a relationship is not 'words' but 'actions'!

31

The best way to add 'color' and 'variety' to your relationship is to let the other person be himself or herself!

32

The 'need to be heard' is a universal need. When you simply listen, you simply improve the quality of your relationship!

<u>33</u>

Relationships are like grains of sand in your hand. Held loosely with love and freedom, they remain. Held tightly with control and restriction, they slip away!

34

Without the fragrance of appreciation, a relationship becomes stale. Keep it fragrant with appreciation!

35

Your role in a relationship is not to get the other person interested in you. Your role is to become interested in the other person!

36

Perfection is an illusion of the ego. Let go the illusion, and see your relationship become more perfect!

37

You play your 'true' role in a relationship when the other person's happiness becomes as important to you, as your own!

<u>38</u>

There can be no relationship when one person wins and the other loses. Always think Win-Win!

<u>39</u>

You cannot be
'everything to everyone'
but you could be
'something to someone'
in a relationship!

<u>40</u>

As the sun melts away ice, kindness melts away misgivings in a relationship!

<u>41</u>

Sorrows shared in a
relationship are halfed
and Joys shared are
doubled!

42

Be careful of the walls you build in your relationship. They could soon become your lonely prison!

43

Just as fire purifies gold, difficult times purify relationships. Allow the fire of difficult times, to make your relationship golden!

44

People may forget what you said to them in a relationship. They'll never forget how you made them feel!

45

Alone, you are One.

Together, you are a Team!

46

A long road never feels long in good company. This is the best secret to a long-lasting relationship!

47

Like the morning light peels away the darkness of the night, a sunny smile is often all it takes to peel away the darkness of a strained relationship!

48

When you find true joy
and happiness in the
expression of the other
person's best qualities
and talents, you make the
relationship a true abode
of love and happiness!

49

A relationship is a new world waiting to explored and enjoyed. How much of it you explore and enjoy it is totally up to you!

50

Remember, 'Words' and 'actions' are building blocks that build trust in your relationship!

51

Care is the ingredient that makes your relationship most flavorful!

<u>52</u>

The feeling of 'oneness' and 'togetherness' is what everyone craves. Find ways to bolster those feelings in your relationship!

53

Difficult times test the strength of your relationship. Without them, you'll never know, how strong your relationship is!

<u>54</u>

In a 'Loving' relationship

'Love' is your only choice!

55

Quality relationships require quality time. Spend quality time to show each other you 'care'!

56

People in the 'best' of relationships, are people who are 'best' friends!

57

Keep the 'excitements' alive in your relationship by keeping the 'surprises' alive!

<u>58</u>

Treat your relationship like the most beautiful and amazing thing on this planet, if you want it to be, the most beautiful and amazing thing!

59

Be honest and truthful in your relationship. There are no substitutes for honesty and truthfulness!

<u>60</u>

A relationship is a performance stage for two souls, seeking expression of each other's divine luminance!

<u>61</u>

Conversations are like food you serve in your relationship. Keep them healthy and tasty!

<u>62</u>

When you truly love someone, you'll make every effort to make them happy!

63

People in great

relationships focus on

'solutions' not 'problems'!

64

You choose 'monotony' over 'variety' when you try to change someone to become like you. What you need in a relationship is 'variety' not 'monotony'!

65

Your goal in a relationship should be, to make a difference in a person's life and not your own!

66

Realize how good your relationship is when things are together, before it is too late to realize, after things fall apart!

67

Without relationships, you'll have no one to share your love!

<u>68</u>

A true relationship can only be built and never be 'bought'. Build it with your devoted 'time' and 'attention'!

69

No one can read your mind or know your feelings. Make sure to let the person in your relationship know, what you are thinking and how you are feeling!

<u>70</u>

The more passion and ideas you bring to your relationship, the richer and more abundant it becomes!

71

When you make a
person feel 'wanted' in a
relationship, you will
become the most
'wanted' person!

72

Keep your relationship constantly renewed by letting go the 'old' and letting in the 'new'!

73

When you choose 'love' over 'hate' during difficult times in a relationship, you choose 'miracle' over 'misery'!

74

What matters most in a relationship is 'affection' not 'perfection'!

75

A relationship is like a home. When something stops working, you don't buy a new home. You fix what's not working!

76

The greatest joys of life are beautiful memories you create in relationships!

77

Be the person in your relationship who will be 'remembered' forever and not the person who will be forever 'forgotten'!

78

Relationships are nothing but a reflection of your own inner world. If you don't like what you see, fix your inner world instead of fixing the reflection!

79

Instead of looking for a 'good' person to have a relationship, be the 'good' person you are looking for!

<u>80</u>

Few moments spent together in love is better than several moments spent apart!

81

Complete acceptance

makes a relationship

'Complete'!

<u>82</u>

Explore the 'unknown' and 'what your relationship could be', instead of being stuck with the 'known' and 'what has always been'!

83

Great relationships are great not because they do not have 'problems', they are great because they have 'solutions'!

<u>84</u>

Engage in open and loving conversations, to keep the joy and fun flowing in your relationship!

85

Continue to do what you did, when you first fell in love and see your relationship continue forever and never end!

86

You become deserving
of what you seek, when
you give what you seek!

<u>87</u>

Appreciate similarities and accept differences in your relationship, to transform it into a beautiful haven of love and understanding!

88

Make every moment you spend with someone; the best moment of their life and they will be yours forever!

89

A true relationship has

a beginning but no

ending!

<u>90</u>

When you love someone for who they are, you will be loved for who you are!

91

Just like flowers need light to blossom, relationships need love. When you shine the light of love in your relationship, it will blossom beyond your wildest dreams!

92

Learn to value 'people' more than 'things' in your relationships. 'Things' become meaningless without the people!

93

Your heart sees more than your eyes. Deeper your heart sees, deeper your relationship becomes!

<u>94</u>

A relationship is like a game of cards. You need the whole set of cards, with all the different shapes, colors and symbols, to play and enjoy to the fullest!

95

A relationship is not like an occasional breeze that comes and goes, it's like the air that maybe silent but always there!

96

In a true relationship,

you don't try to be happy.
Happiness just happens!

<u>97</u>

You start a relationship by 'falling in love'. You keep it by 'staying in love'!

98

Be in a relationship not because you 'need' the person. Be in it because you 'love' the person!

99

Needs make a relationship 'selfish'. Love makes it 'selfless'!

<u>100</u>

Keep the peace in your relationship at all cost. It's the life blood of your relationship!

101

How you make a person 'feel', matters more than what you 'say' or 'do' in a relationship!

102

If there is any room for pride in a relationship, it's pride for the other person and not yourself!

103

It's easy to 'get' something you easily 'give' in a relationship!

<u>104</u>

Genuine 'care' is the heart of a loving relationship. Without 'care' there is no relationship!

105

Love 'shared' multiplies Joy. Love 'withheld' multiplies suffering!

106

Relationships flourish when you accept a person's past, care about their present and support their future!

107

When someone tells you, you hurt them in a relationship. It's not the time for you to defend your actions. It's time for you to do what is necessary to make the feelings right!

108

A relationship is like a garden. The more you water and tend to it, the more beautiful it becomes!

109

A 'loving heart' and a 'helping hand' is the hallmark of a great relationship!

110

Smiles add miles to relationships. Smile together more often!

111

The more truly you love someone, the more truly you taste Love!

<u>112</u>

When you love someone truly, every hour, minute and second of your life becomes truly timeless and eternal!

113

You are together with someone today because, it was meant to be and could not be any other way!

114

When you fall in love with someone, you don't discover the person - You discover yourself!

115

Small acts of love you
show in a relationship,
shows the other person,
small parts of them they
never knew existed!

116

Open new and exciting possibilities by saying 'Yes' more often in your relationship!

<u>117</u>

The most important person in the world right now, is the person you are with, right now!

<u>118</u>

Pay attention to what you 'do' in a relationship. Your actions always speak louder than your words!

<u>119</u>

If you love someone ...

Say it!

Show it!

Be it!

<u>120</u>

The best way to love someone, is not by changing them, but by helping them become the best version of themselves!

<u>121</u>

Life is a vast ocean of love and relationships are meant to be beautiful expressions of this ocean!

122

Great friendships always build great relationships!

123

Remember, what you don't do matters as much as what you do in a relationship!

124

When you give willingly with your heart expecting nothing in return, you enjoy the purest form of love in your relationship!

125

It's best to avoid making

mistakes in a relationship.
But, if you do, it's best to
never repeat them!

126

When you have nothing to hide, you'll have nothing to fear in a relationship!

127

A good relationship does not just happen - You make it happen!

128

The best apology in a relationship is not what you say - it's what you do after you apologize!

129

Strong people lift people up and weak people put people down. Be the strong person in your relationship!

130

An argument is not worth winning, if it ends up costing you a good relationship!

<u>131</u>

If you wait for someone to change to be happy, you'll probably wait your entire life!

<u>132</u>

Focus on things you can change in your relationship instead of focusing on things you cannot change!

133

You are never too young or old, to dream new dreams and try new things in a relationship!

134

Always remember this relationship rule: Listen before you speak, think before you act, wait before you criticize and try before you give up!

<u>135</u>

Just like your past actions determined the present state of your relationship, your present actions will determine it's future state!

<u>136</u>

Choose a gentler approach to discussing problems instead of blame, attack or criticism. The way you discuss problems in your relationship, not only determines how your conversations will go, it also determines how your relationship will go!

137

Instead of always trying to fix broken things in your relationship, try to start things over to create something better!

138

Never complain about yesterday in your relationship. It can neither make your today nor your tomorrow better!

139

It's not often the big things that make a big difference in your relationship but the small things!

140

A relationship is the coming together of two beautiful souls to create one beautiful world!

<u>141</u>

Focus on *'what you want'*, instead of *'what you don't want'*. You'll get what you focus on, regardless of whether you want it or not!

<u>142</u>

Don't take yourself too seriously - A relationship is not about you, it's about the other person!

143

A perfect relationship is where two people come together to love each other, knowing they are not perfect and work together, to create a imperfectly perfect world they both love!

144

Remember, a relationship is better off without the person, who is incapable of making it better, by being in it!

145

Success in a relationship is not measured by how much your life is enhanced by the relationship. It's measured by how much the relationship is enhanced by you!

<u>146</u>

Ignoring each other's emotional needs can drain a relationship emotionally. Attend to the emotional needs in your relationship by making each other feel heard and loved!

<u>147</u>

Frank and open communication is a great way to deepen and strengthen a relationship. Compliment and vocalize your feelings for each other and also be willing to talk about things that may seem bad or uncomfortable!

<u>148</u>

A relationship needs respect just like plants need water. When you keep your relationship watered with respect, you'll see it grow and flourish like you never imagined!

149

The quality of connection in your relationship, depends on the quality of time spent and not on the quantity of time!

<u>150</u>

Complete dependence on someone for all your needs, is a recipe for unhappiness in a relationship. Learn to manage both independence and interdependence wisely, to keep your relationship happy!

151

Tell each other what makes you feel loved and special instead of silently expecting to feel loved and special. Clarifying expectations makes attending to each other's needs easy!

152

The happiest people have no time comparing their relationship with others. They are busy making their own relationship happy!

<u>153</u>

A 'full-filled'
relationship requires two
people giving their 'full'
100%!

<u>154</u>

The greatest gift you can give someone in life is a joyful relationship. The greatest gift you can give yourself, is also a joyful relationship!

155

When you genuinely understand each other, your relationship become a genuine haven of understanding!

156

The foundation of a strong relationship is the feeling you instill that, you'll always be there for the person - no matter what, when and where!

157

Unconditional love transforms a relationship into a temple of divine love and healing!

<u>158</u>

Make it a habit to share the trivialities of life to refuel warmth and connection in your relationship. The simple act itself is more important than the specifics of what you share!

159

Great relationships are your greatest assets on this planet - protect and preserve them at all cost!

160

You'll truly enjoy your relationships, when you truly enjoy bringing out the best in the other person!

161

Listening to each other's needs and concerns without judgment, is often, all it takes to solve problems in your relationship!

<u>162</u>

The least you can do in a relationship is - to simply be there for the person when they need you!

163

The depth of your relationship is not measured by its length. It's measured by the breadth of your love!

164

The best way to know love is to love someone!

165

Without good relationships, you could be a lonely person in a lonely world!

166

You are the artist in your relationship. Each day, presents new opportunities, to create beautiful master pieces!

167

Have no other purpose in a relationship other than, to enhance and enrich it!

168

A relationship without the foundation of genuine love, will not last the test of time!

169

Loving relationships will
never lose value, beauty
or go out of style!

170

You give meaning to everything in your relationship, just as with everything in life. Remember, it's not the other person's fault, if you choose to give something the wrong meaning!

171

When you forget everything, you give and remember everything you receive in a relationship, gratefulness becomes your only choice!

172

Nothing happens in a relationship by accident. Everything happens by choice. When you make the right choices, there will be no accidents!

173

Treat the person in your relationship, the way you like to be treated - Nothing more, nothing less!

174

An open and loving relationship can happen only with an open and loving heart!

<u>175</u>

True measure of success in your relationship is not always the number of things you have to discuss every day but the number of things you no longer have to discuss every day!

176

When you truly cherish each other's hopes and dreams, your relationship becomes something to be truly cherished!

177

Instead of looking for a loving relationship your whole life. Dedicate your whole life for a loving relationship!

178

Arguments reveal 'truths' in your relationship which could be used as stepping stones to take your relationship to the next level!

179

When you make yourself available in times of need, you make yourself worthy of a good relationship!

180

When you keep the 'honesty' in your relationship, you'll honestly keep it successful!

181

An extra ordinary relationship is one in which, two people come together to make ordinary things extra ordinary!

182

A true relationship is

your commitment to -
Desire the highest good
for a person for the rest
of your life!

183

One of the best gifts you can give a person in a relationship is - The gift of undivided attention!

184

You make a relationship better, when you make the person's life better!

185

A good relationship is a commitment to always be there for the person, even though, you may not always be there with the person!

186

A true relationship is not about what's convenient for you. It's about what's convenient for the other person!

187

You can either make yourself 'happy' or 'unhappy' in a relationship. Remember, making yourself 'happy' is far easier than making yourself unhappy'!

188

The best way to build closeness in relationship is, to provide a safe place for each other to share your feelings!

<u>189</u>

A good relationship is not about having the best relationship every single day. It's about building a better relationship with every passing day!

190

'Nothing' in this world is worth more than the 'peace' in your relationship. Let 'no-thing' take away your peace!

191

A strong relationship does not require two people to be strong all the time. It only requires one person to be strong when the other is weak!

<u>192</u>

A great relationship does not happen between two people who think they are two. It happens between two people who think they are one!

193

The best way to understand a person is not with your head but with your heart!

194

When you feel love for a person, you don't feel the person, you feel your own true self as the other person!

195

It's amazing how loving someone, can put you in touch with your own essence!

196

It's not the other

person's job to make you happy. The only person who can make you happy is - YOU!

197

You can see, hear, smell, taste and touch beautiful things. However, the only way you can feel their beauty is - With your heart!

198

You were born to love and to be loved. Life gave you relationships...to love and to be loved!

199

You will simply be happy, when you simply make someone happy!

200

The simplest way to multiply your happiness is by simply sharing it!

201

Every moment in a relationship, is a doorway to make your unfulfilled 'dreams' a 'reality'!

202

It's not about 'who' is right in any given moment in a relationship. It's about 'what' is right in any given moment!

203

Healthy relationships keep your mind and body in better health than any exercise at a Health Club!

204

Don't let the grind of everyday life get the better of your relationship. Let your relationship get the better of your everyday grind!

205

Don't expect your relationship to be like any other, because, you are two unique people. Expect it to be unique and enjoy its uniqueness!

206

'Small' acts of kindness you do every day make can a 'Big' difference in your relationship!

207

An apology does not necessarily mean you did something wrong. It means, you are doing what is necessary to make something right!

208

One moment of selfless love can change one moment of your life. A lifetime of selfless love can change your entire life!

209

When you become more aware of your feelings and feelings of others, you can consciously manage your own emotions and the overall flow of E-Motion (Energy in Motion) in your relationships!

210

How you feel within yourself profoundly impacts the state of your relationship. Learn to bring yourself back quickly into a state of feeling good, whenever you find yourself drifting into a state of feeling bad!

211

A great relationship is not about falling in love with a person once. It's about falling in love with a person every single day!

212

That which changes is not real. Keep your relationship 'real' with steadfast and unwavering love!

213

You can most definitely make your reality better than your dreams if: You have the courage, to take your dreams and turn them into something better!

214

If heaven is a place of unconditional love, your relationship can become a 'heavenly' place with unconditional love!

215

If you expect your relationship to be good every single day, consider how much good, you are contributing to it, every single day!

<u>216</u>

When someone loves you deeply, they reveal their highest self to you. When you love someone deeply, you reveal your highest self to them. A relationship is the only place on this planet where you can reveal your highest self to someone every single day!

217

You will live fully, only

when you love fully!

218

Success in a relationship is not determined by the number of promises you make. It is determined by the number of promises you keep!

219

You should love someone not because of who they are. You should love someone because of who you are!

220

If people could die for someone in a relationship, you could most certainly live for someone in a relationship!

221

Conversations are an important part of a relationship. Find time for face to face personal conversations everyday, instead of always going places or doing things that involve little or no talking or listening!

<u>222</u>

Put all your body, mind and soul into your relationship. The universe put all of itself into bringing you together!

223

The best relationship is one where you awaken a person's soul and make them want to reach out for more!

224

There can only be two basic motivations in a relationship: Fear and Love. Fear closes your heart and love opens it, to all the joy, excitement and possibilities, waiting to blossom in your relationship!

<u>225</u>

Without true love, life and relationships have no true meaning!

<u>226</u>

When you understand the power of love in a relationship, the love of power loses it's power over you!

<u>227</u>

What matters most in a relationship is, not how it looks from the outside. What matters most is, how it looks from the inside!

228

Your relationship becomes truly interesting only when you become truly interested in the other person!

229

When you share enjoyable experiences together in a relationship, you enhance the connection and make it more enjoyable!

230

The more you move out of your comfort zone and make yourself vulnerable, the more venerable you become in your relationship!

231

You'll get what you've always got in your relationship, if you do what you've always done!

<u>232</u>

A truly open relationship opens up everything that's truly worth living for in this life!

233

Take a mental vacation to be fully present emotionally with your partner every day. This will help build an emotionally strong relationship!

234

Small expressions of gratitude every day will yield big dividends in your relationship!

235

A relationship is a journey and not a destination. Let go your expectation to arrive and enjoy the Journey!

<u>236</u>

Your love for someone

may not change the world
but it may change the
world for someone!

237

What you do for each other every day as expressions of love, is more important than the feelings you have for each other in your relationship!

238

You become capable of truly loving someone, when you become capable of truly loving yourself!

239

When you do new and exciting things together in a relationship, you keep it renewed and exciting!

240

To create fulfilling relationships is part of your own responsibility to create a fulfilling life!

241

Having mutual goals or projects you can work on together in a relationship, gives you a sense of pride, achievement and team spirit!

242

You are a team of two unique individuals bringing different perspectives and strengths to your relationship. Remember, the value you both bring to your relationship are — Your Differences!

243

When someone in a relationship does something, make sure to talk about it and explore why he or she is doing it, without making any assumptions!

<u>244</u>

Your ability to handle and manage differences in your relationship, is what makes all the difference!

<u>245</u>

Don't let problems and bitterness simmer in your relationship. Resolve them when they happen and don't let them to boil over!

246

Be careful of what you sow in your relationship. Sooner or later, you will reap what you sow!

247

In the absence of 'closeness', people often fall out of love. Maintain the 'closeness' in your relationship, through regular care and attention!

248

Never undermine a good relationship by underestimating the power of good grooming!

249

Your willingness to apologize and make up after an argument is very vital for the happiness of your relationship!

250

Spending time 'apart' doing your own things independently is equally as important as spending time 'together' in a relationship!

251

It's easier to have a good relationship with someone, when you have a good relationship with yourself. Always, nurture and maintain a sense of good self-respect and self-esteem!

<u>252</u>

Relationships exist for Love and Love exists for relationships!

253

A relationship is a two-way street. That's the only way it's designed work — with a lot of give and take!

254

Always stay open to spontaneity and allow room for surprises in your relationship!

<u>255</u>

Good physical, mental and emotional health is required to enjoy a healthy relationship. Do everything possible to stay physically, mentally and emotionally healthy!

256

All relationships have their ups and downs and don't always ride at a continuous high. Learning to ride the high and low tides together, makes your relationship stronger!

257

Use your relationships as a mirror to see yourself and understand things within you, that cause things, you like or dislike in your relationship!

258

A relationship is complete only when there is complete freedom for the people involved!

259

Share laughter in your relationship to keep it lively and vibrant. The playful energy of laughter alleviates stress and fosters a greater sense of togetherness!

<u>260</u>

A real relationship is never perfect and a perfect relationship is never real!

261

Love is not an absolute or finite commodity you give and take in a relationship. It's the endless ocean of Life and the purest essence of all Existence. How much of it finds expression in your life, depends on how much of it, you are willing to express through you!

Wishing you the very

best of life, filled with the

most wonderful, loving,

fulfilling, joyful and

enduring relationships!

With Love

Roy John

NOTES

<u>NOTES</u>

NOTES

<u>NOTES</u>

NOTES